Birth Story Brave
A Guide for Reflecting on Your Childbirth Experience

EMILY SOUDER, LCSW-C

Copyright © 2017 Emily Souder

This guide is not meant as a replacement for psychotherapy or working through
birth-related topics with a professional. The reader should consult a physician or a
mental health professional in matters relating to his/her mental health and
particularly with respect to any symptoms that may require diagnosis or medical
attention.

Cover design and interior graphics by C&V Creative

Cover photo by Sergei Mironenko

Edited by Jodi Brandon Editorial

Author photo by Stevie T Photography

First Edition

ISBN-13: 978-0-692-98240-2

DEDICATION

This guide is dedicated to Momma. Thank you for allowing me to be part of your story, and for giving creativity a space in my heart..

ACKNOWLEDGMENTS

There were so many people who were helpful throughout the process of dreaming up and creating this guide. Thanks to my husband for listening to my original vision and believing in it for the entire ride. Thanks to Val and Emily for reading through my first draft and providing such valuable, honest feedback. Thanks to Jodi for being a knowledgeable editor and confident presence. Thanks to Illiah for being attentive to my style and creating such a gorgeous cover. Thanks to Stevie for capturing images that made me feel beautiful, even if I felt awkward inside! And of course, thanks to all of the mamas who have trusted me with their stories. I am so grateful.

CONTENTS

PREFACE

This guide is intended to serve as a loving, gentle tool to assist moms with processing their birth story after the birth of one or more children. The questions refer to one birth *experience*, but allow for the fact that some births result in multiple babies! The reader is able to revisit these questions as many times as she desires to apply them to different birth experiences.

The guide is separated into four sections: Starting, Progressing, Meeting Your Baby, and After. The sections and questions follow the progression of birth from the beginning of labor until after the baby (or babies!) has been born. The reader is able to pick up and put down the guide as many times as she wishes; there is no required pace. Choose the rhythm that feels right to you and try not to force anything you're not ready to visit. And, of course, remember to show compassion for yourself.

INTRODUCTION

Pivotal life moments leave lasting impressions. We process them, or fail to process them, we often make meaning about them, and we create narratives about them. Birthing a child or children is an example of such a moment in our lives. It doesn't matter how your baby or babies passed from you into the world (vaginally or via cesarean section). This story is sacred. What story have you been telling yourself about your child's birth—that wedge of time when your child spent their last moments within your body and first moments outside of you?

Birth stories are not always clean, straightforward, and joyful. They can be messy, complex, and sometimes mixed with pain. It serves us well to give a voice to all sides of the story, not just the parts that we feel we "should" have. It's okay to feel loss *and* excitement, grief *and* awe. This guide creates a path for you to explore your story, to turn it over and examine it as you would a rock. Be curious. Find a beautiful journal in which you can pen your responses. You may choose to share your journaling with others, or you may not. That's up to you.

I invite you to write down your birth story in its entirety, either together with your responses to these prompts or elsewhere. Authentically reviewing the details can help us process the event and, plus, it will document information that might otherwise get lost in our memories.

It goes without saying that the questions I pose will not touch all areas of your story, but my hope is that they will open a pathway for you to explore. Follow the questions where they lead. Be brave. Look into yourself and tune in. Hear the voice asking for a listening ear.

You have a story to tell, Mama. Let's walk this path together. I invite you to leave judgment at the door. Get comfy, and let's begin.

SNAILS?

During the period of time I was thinking about and planning this project, snail shells and snails seemed to follow me around. Way more than enough to catch my attention. I've always liked snails, but I'd only seen a handful of them in person over the course of my lifetime. All of a sudden, upon the birth of this project, they were *everywhere*. Shells upon shells that had washed up on the beach, tiny friends visiting our garden, and even ones right on my front porch as I walked through my front door.

I am often one to look to animals for messages when they appear so purposely in my life, and this situation was no different. I read about snails and the reminder they give to slow down. I came back to that message again and again throughout the publishing of *Birth Story Brave*. Slow down, let it happen, don't rush it.

The shells themselves seem to carry even deeper meaning, and some believe they can represent the life cycle, fertility, and change. Even without these meanings attached, there is something about that beautiful shape. It seems to invite us to be still and reflect.

So, the spirals and snail messengers needed a place in this book. Let them remind you as well to take it slow and pause.

AN IMPORTANT NOTE

This guide is not meant as a replacement for psychotherapy or working through birth-related topics with a professional. However, it can of course be used as a tool within the context of such work.

If you are having difficulty adjusting to your new role in parenthood, are having symptoms of depression and anxiety, or feel that you are having a hard time connecting to your little one, please don't hesitate to seek professional help with working through it. Also, if you notice that journaling about your experience triggers a strong reaction that feels scary to you, don't be afraid or embarrassed to ask for help. More mamas have been there than you know. Postpartum Support International (www.postpartum.net) and Postpartum Stress Center (www.postpartumstress.com) are great places to start looking for resources.

SECTION 1: STARTING

.

One

This is the moment when you knew for sure: I'm going to meet my baby or babies today (or at least in the coming days, if your story lasts longer!). Close your eyes and remember. What was your first thought when you realized that was a "real" contraction, or when you woke up on the day of your scheduled cesarean section? Or maybe the birth of your little one(s) took you by complete surprise, and you didn't have much time to think ahead. Wherever your story starts is okay. Reflect on it now.

Two

At the beginning, what hopes were you bringing into this experience with you? What fears were there?

Three

How did you feel about your body and what it was about to go through? Were you feeling strong and capable? Uncertain? Weak? What was your body telling you?

Four

At this point, what did you imagine your baby might be experiencing?

Five

What did the environment around you feel like? Peaceful? Chaotic? Energized? Did this work for you?

Six

How did you cope with any feelings of uncertainty? Did you rely on those around you? An inner mantra? Meditation or distraction?

Seven

Close your eyes and picture yourself at this part in your story. What image comes to mind? It doesn't have to be a snapshot of the actual event. Maybe you see something different, like an animal or colors. What does this represent to you?

Eight

Look back over the pages you have written in this section. Have any themes emerged? Place your hand over your heart and take several deep breaths. What do you notice? What, if anything, can you release or forgive? If you sense any judgment, give yourself permission to let it go, and exhale. Invite in love and understanding—the kind you would extend to your very best friend.

SECTION 2: PROGRESSING

One

The journey has intensified. You're in labor, working through strong contractions, not knowing how long this will continue. Or maybe you're about to go into an operating room, uncertain of what lies ahead. Every mama's story is different.

You are in the midst of your birth journey. What are your senses saying to you at this point in the story?

Two

Who is around you? What is their energy like? What is the general feeling of the environment around you? Are you aware of things outside of yourself? It's very possible that you may have been too focused on the task at hand to be paying any attention to external qualities.

Three

Are there things that happened at this point that you didn't like? Things that felt wrong or out of alignment to you? Especially if you had developed a carefully constructed birth plan, or even if you didn't, anything different from what you had envisioned might not sit well. For example, did you feel pressured to stay in one position when you wanted to walk around, or did you not have the options you wanted for pain control?

Four

Were there any moments during this time when you felt particularly proud of yourself? Take time to recognize your courage and strength.

Five

What might you be able to let go of? What still feels unfinished?

SECTION 3: MEETING YOUR BABY

One

You worked so hard, Mama. This is not always a time of pure happiness; it can be mixed. Maybe there is some lingering fear or anxiety. It's all okay. Remember: This is *your* story. Here, no one can tell you your feelings are out of place. You're safe.

What were your first thoughts after your baby was/babies were born?

Two

Which emotions were present for you at this time? No judgment is needed; you felt what you felt.

Three

Are there any physical sensations that you remember?

Four

What feels sacred about these first moments with your baby or babies? If nothing does, that's okay. Reflect on that, too. Did something feel out of place?

Five

Were these first post-birth moments what you expected? How did they feel different? How did they feel aligned?

SECTION 4: AFTER

One

Let's talk about expectations. Our vision of something, before we experience it, can be vastly different from the reality of living it. What were your expectations of birth? How did they differ from reality? Is this something that is difficult for you to move beyond?

Two

Similarly, what beliefs did you have about birth before going through it? How, if at all, has your perspective changed?

Three

What victories or celebrations do you have around your birth story? When might you have felt empowered? Strong?

Four

Look within yourself. Are you holding any feelings of regret? Where are they lingering in your story?

Five

Choose some words to describe your birth story, after having been able to reflect. It's okay if you don't feel all of them are positive. It's your story, and it's real, and it's all allowed.

Six

If you were to choose a title for your birth story, what would it be? Go with whatever feels right. Use humor, if you'd like!

Seven

Is there an epilogue to your birth story? Think about what might be presented in this section. Carry this forward. Think about how you will relay your child's birth story from now on. What will you tell your child or children?

GRATITUDE

I am so glad you chose to explore this part of yourself. Thank you for letting me walk this path with you. Your story is important, but please don't let it hold you back or define you. Simply thank it and show gratitude for it, as it is one of the many pieces that will come together to shape who you are becoming. Don't let this guide be the end of your exploration, either. Keep this momentum going! You will be given many opportunities for growth and advancement, so don't be afraid to listen when they speak to you.

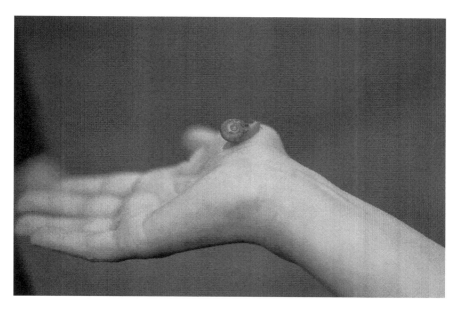

Photo by Stevie T Photography

ABOUT THE AUTHOR

Emily Souder is a licensed clinical social worker who has a passion for working with pregnant women and postpartum mamas who are challenged by adjustment concerns, anxiety, depression, and other maternal mental health difficulties. She is a proud wife and mother of two (and a dog!) who aims to remain inspired by the day-to-day—but who knows we're human, and, well, some days just don't feel so inspired! Emily and her family live in Maryland.

66576221R00029

Made in the USA
Middletown, DE
13 March 2018